Gaps
Jenny Danes

smith|doorstop

Published 2017 by
smith|doorstop books
The Poetry Business
Bank Street Arts
32-40 Bank Street
Sheffield S1 2DS

Copyright © Jenny Danes 2017
All Rights Reserved

ISBN 978-1-910367-97-1
Typeset by Utter
Author photo: Laura Beresford Photography
Printed by Biddles

Acknowledgements
Thanks are due to the editors of *The North*, *The Rialto* and *The Kindling*, in which some of these poems or versions of them have appeared.

'Notes on Missing a Person' was highly commended in the Bridport Prize in 2016.

Thanks to The Poetry Business and The Writing Squad for their continued encouragement and support. Particular heartfelt thanks go to Helen Mort and Stevie Ronnie for their invaluable help, and to Emma Danes and Daisy Behagg for their insightful readings of early versions of some of these poems.

smith|doorstop books are a member of Inpress:
www.inpressbooks.co.uk. Distributed by Central Books Ltd.,
99 Wallis Road, London E9 5LN

The Poetry Business gratefully acknowledges the support
of Arts Council England.

Contents

5	Moving to another country
6	November
7	Your House
8	Wire
9	Names
10	Shower
11	Inked
12	Sing
13	Flies
15	This is what it feels like
17	Nikolaus
18	Gaps
19	Notes on Missing a Person
20	Kiwis
21	Trains
22	Things I Left in Germany
23	Deutsch

Moving to another country

is like paddling on rough beaches
where the waves plough and drag stones

from under your feet – the unsteadying
rush of it, a sharp sinking.

From my sand-filled mouth
clauses trip and fall.

I make three faux pas in a row
that are all to do with drinking,

and a stranger tells me I can't
pronounce my R's properly.

I go out to dinner with new friends
and am the only one with a boring name.

Crossing the street, I look the wrong way
and two cyclists slam my heart

into my mouth. Sometimes people
ask me for the English word, and I can't think.

I've put poetry in a box somewhere.
Darkness comes and holds me like a glove,

which, by next morning, is a fist.

November

Anxiety uncoils itself and stretches as wide and hollow
as the unfamiliar sky. I fall in, and today is lost.
The morning is dull and a sort of heavy white, as if the day crept up unexpectedly
and shouldn't really be here at all. I am scraped out on the inside.
Old Bavarian men glance at me and smoke and mutter things,
this mad English girl crying on the phone. It gets later and more people
begin to trickle out from around corners. They look composed,
purposeful, normal. I sit on a slightly damp rock and stare
at a tree standing in its own debris, leaves skittered out
like children sitting in a circle. When I was seven my teacher told
the whole class *I like the way Jennifer tried to spell 'anxious'*
and the leaves at the back giggled and I learned the definition if not
the spelling. I tilt my head and try and think of a word that scoops them up
but all I can conclude is they're not beautiful or bright, just dead,
the sort of leaves you'd crush to dust rather than paint.
I am so tired and so inappropriately placed. People look at me
and I look at the dark constant earth, damp and welcoming.
If the words on every sign are strange, should you just shut your eyes?
What about failing to eavesdrop and putting on headphones? What about love?
If we can't survive being buried in each other's mother tongue
maybe we should abandon the rest, close our hearts and mouths

Your House

The thoughts are like huge men bursting
into every room. They put their feet up
on the kitchen table and stare. Their hands
are on your things; their faces are masked.
You can't just ask them to leave.

After the first two or three men,
you seem to invite more.
You can't help yourself.
You shrink against an upstairs wall
and give up your house.

Next morning the thoughts fade
and become part of the furniture.
A particularly burly man
becomes your writing desk.
Some men slip into the dust on the bookshelves.

Others will be mirrors, bannisters,
picture frames. Two of the largest
become bedposts, crouching
at the end of your room,
their shadows growing every night.

Wire

I am not allowed to talk about the heart
      because it is too visceral
           and too red
and also too much like syrup. Instead
I shall call mine a wire sculpture
     of a bird's nest   built very carefully
           inside my ribs,
and whenever anything gets too close
   there's that hair-raising sound
of rubbed metal,   like the awkwardness
of badly hung towels
        or of the way I slept
the first night you were gone.
With a sculpture you can achieve a sense of ringing
        all through your body.
   Whatever you are feeling,
     I can get twists of metal to echo
all the way
           down to my toes.
  Any sadness is always in tune.
I used to want
    to be the microscopic
                      specks
and ridges in paper
   I wanted
       to be in a book
  but only as a tiny fibre deep in the crease,
now I want to be an atom,
blind and
    buried   in my metal
   I could stay cold and hard and ringing
and there would be no need for you

Names

I met my boyfriend at a train station. He leaned over to hear my name and then told me his with such matter-of- fact confidence, a sort of bluntness I couldn't help admiring, as if it was a perfectly good, maybe even ideal name, and nobody could possibly have a problem with it or with him. It was a name I'd only previously come across in our German textbooks at school; I nodded sort of dazedly that of course it was a real name here, a good, typical name; here he was, my first proof. I read recently that you should say your name with love and pride, otherwise people will look back at you and say 'I didn't catch that', because it is indeed something you must throw, accurately, a beautiful little launch from the tongue. Why, then, do I struggle with the mere two syllables of mine, the vowel emerging ambiguous, the double N getting stuck, the whole thing sounding too high or too quiet – or, when I try for the opposite, too bold, as if I'm thrusting my name in their face, eyes locking theirs and blood warming my cheeks just hoping they will hear, accept, nod, smile; again and again I throw my name and in the frozen half-second when it is heard I play it back again and again and grow hot, waiting, eyes fixed and saying know me, know me.

Shower

It's beautiful because   it's not sexual
   it's human   and clumsy   and there's love

you use my shampoo   and I wash your back
I have the gift of your form   the inches I've not seen before

the way your arm hair turns   dark and matted
   the small of your back   the gaps between your toes.

Under the water I am   trapped and therefore
opened to you   mouth and eyes flooded

not seeing or speaking   but knowing
you're looking at my face   with such simple   boldness

in a moment when nobody's   looked at it
before.   The shower is the strangeness

of reclaiming a body as your own   after joining it with another
   of losing   the sweet animal smell
                              of the night

Inked

I want to enter your language naked
and roll around until I'm covered in it,

skin stained with vocabulary
dense enough to turn me dark,

nouns dripping from the ends of my hair,
verbs flooding my mouth.

I'll leave the ink to work
into my bloodstream

or else stand in the rain,
let it stream black off me,

every possible sentence
pooling at my feet.

Sing

It's not romantic. There's something desperate,
half-violent in the way we move.
Our bodies fill the gap our language leaves.

The next morning is lonely and my flesh
sings a slightly different tune.
I've had enough of my own form,

heavy as a sack, this tongue, this skin
still strange from your touch,
a tuning fork's keen quiver –

I'm becoming my own light source,
the air around me sharp
and bright, its surface broken
like a note just struck.

Flies

I'm having thoughts again and they
come in, sensing I don't know what,

maybe it's warm in here, or I smell good,
maybe anxiety smells good,

or I left something sticky on the worktop.
They land on me and buzz suddenly

in my left ear and crawl across my desk
rubbing their little legs together.

I've had an episode and he comes round.
He jokes about my eyes, asking about allergies.

Before we go to bed, we kill a fly.
It takes us nearly an hour.

He shuts me in the bathroom with it
and lies tea towels under the door so it can't get out.

I'm holding a rolled up magazine
and keep flinching. It's quicker than me.

In the end I drown it in the shower.
I feel worse after watching it die

and slip down the drain
than I'd done all evening.

That night I'm afraid of every noise
and thoughts are circles in my head

and I keep picturing that dead fly
small and black, floating just out of sight.

This is what it feels like

I

Considering I have become a wall,
my heart is beating curiously
fast

The wall is very cold

I can't decide whether it's glass or
concrete but it doesn't matter

What matters is it's untouchable, unpatterned

and hard to breathe through

What's left of my old body
is just lots of water

II

I've been thinking about soil
proper moist rich dark soil

and how I'd like to put my face in it
it would be so cool against

my closed eyelids
it would smell reliable

the heavy dampness would appeal
(the soil and I would understand each other)

I might do this for real
I want to be unclean

III

I hate hearing the front door go because
something inside me will flinch
Often when I get off the tube,
a man on the other side of the doors
gestures with his hand to sweep me to one side
Everyone is dying, obviously
A man on the street says God bless
even though I didn't give him anything
People have children because they want children
They do not think about whether children want themselves
People are very ignorant
I'm not really exempting myself from that
There is too much that demands to be cared about
Sleeping is not making any difference

IV

I've been thinking about the coast
and how maybe it would help me if I went
and froze my face in the salt-spiked
air and let my heels sink into wet

sand and learned to breathe without
using my upper chest and learned to
breathe under water and learned
to breathe without breathing

Nikolaus

You set down two satsumas on my bedside table:
Nikolaus day. I let you tell me about sweets in shoes,

shaken ash, sticks and coal, while I fuss
over milk and cups and what I'm going to say

when you've finished talking.
You should have seen me during the build-up.

Pacing, straightening covers, practicing German in my head.
You forget your watch and I find it later

under my pillow. I take its handsome weight in my palm
and line it up next to mine, watch the matching hands,

the difference in size and expense. There's blood on the sheets.
I eat Crunchy Nut straight from the box

and feel sad. There's a chill left by your absence.
I sit quietly on the edge of my bed, eat both oranges.

Gaps

Everything is so divided where the sun's cut off
that it looks like someone's peeled back a strip of sky.
A daddy walks his little girl down steps and counts them
eins – zwei - drei - sehr gut. This is what she will learn.
I can't see the lake because the sun is this huge smudge
blinding it out; in fact I can't see anything except the sun
and this is what the prospect of our date feels like.
I can breathe easier out here although fuck my fingers
are really hurting and I do worry and wonder if we will kiss
or more or nothing. Last time we ate and I brushed your hand
and apologised. Now the sky is the colour of parma violets
and the dad and girl are waving at the ducks
although she won't call them ducks. What is this complete
chance that you and I were brought up in different tongues?
How is it that we would name the same object or feeling differently,
and always have done? The gaps come out in my cold breath,
between my teeth, in the groping pauses when I talk –

Notes on Missing a Person

This is his body   written for me
his chin will be the last to go   I know its beard
the way a child knows texture for the first time
top of his chest, yes, but I'm a little vague
about the nipples   stomach, backside, mouth most
definitely   I've lost the legs and hands, to forget his hands
how could I   I know his neck and his freckles
I remember noticing them for the first time
This is my body   it does not know what to do
it is learning what it means to be untouched
it is singing from the rocks   it has no trust in memory
and does not believe he was ever here   it is retreating
to belong only to itself   it is ordinary again
it cannot understand   the lack of him

Kiwis

When we're apart again I find myself eating the things he fed me –
salami, cheese, bread, apples, kiwis – so many kiwis.
He bought us a whole carton, all of them rock hard still,
but we ate them anyway, peeled them with knives:
his ridiculous care not to waste the flesh, almost tender
with his blade, coring out the little white nub at the end.
We feasted on them like peaches, cupped the bare wet flesh,
the sharpness and the seeds and the juice
sudden in our mouths, the joy of it. At home
I sit a packet of six kiwis on my desk
and think of him. They're too ripe to eat this way –
I have to cut them in half and scoop them empty
with a teaspoon: so much sadder, more mechanical,
a process of start to finish. Is it the place,
the lack of his kitchen table, the breadth
and freshness from Italian daylight, of him
setting a fruit down at my place, us sitting,
comfortably quiet, knives scraping careful as woodwork?

Trains

For four days each month
I have two bodies.

The way we join together is warm
and smooth. Even when not touching,

this body is attached to my chest.
It's so normal. We've seen each other

in every possible state. Sometimes
we start to smell like each other.

The body and I slip
between different languages

and between the gaps in our flesh
to the most unknown corners of ourselves.

Then he takes me to the train station
and tears himself away.

My sore chest struggles
to keep up, and my hands don't know what to hold.

I can't understand
how I will not hear, not touch,

smell or taste, how I won't see this body
when I glance up,

and my sadness is a lake,
and its water is in my throat.

Things I Left in Germany

Two pillows, shoes I never wore,
a bath mat, a frying pan,
a blue pot on the bathroom shelf
with an anchor printed on it.
Three broken slats on the bed
and superglue stains.
Also coat hangers, drawing pins,
washing up liquid. My boyfriend.
The next hour of time. A broken
office chair, vacuum bags.
A thicker skin. My signature.
The hob cleaner than when
I first moved in. A few spare Euros
and a nostalgia for England.
A language I'll slowly forget.
The bravest part of myself.

Deutsch

Oh but come and chat out of the little sewing box!
How deep is the sea? I am as happy as a snow king,
I'm on cloud seven, tousled and cosy with my tootle sack –

write that behind your spoon. Blow cake, I was sure I'd be fine
but I'm standing on the hose today. Let's leave the church
in the village. A friend of me interests herself for nozzle beetles.

What goes down? A glow pear, an ice bear, away sickness,
a rain shield, a strike wood to make a flame. In the spring
should the little geese flowers and Easter bells come.

I have the nose painted full. This is a case of the spirit
splitting itself. Yes, exactly, you've met it in the black –
but also shot yourself in the knee. He's got two left hands.

Now we really are sitting in the ink. Nose horn, Nile horse,
belt animal, luck mushroom. I'm speaking in the wind.
I hope this'll conquer your heart in the storm.

Jenny Danes was a winner of the 2015/16 New Poets Prize

The New Poets Prize is a pamphlet competition for writers between the ages of 16 and 22 (inclusive). The prize runs alongside the renowned International Book & Pamphlet Competition organised by The Poetry Business, which has been a staple of the literary calendar since 1986.

Entrants are invited to submit short collections of twelve pages of poems. Four outstanding poets will be selected to receive a year of support and mentoring alongside other prizes, including a place on an Arvon residential course and publication in *The North* magazine.

The winning collections will appear as part of The New Poets List, an imprint of The Poetry Business.

Judging the New Poets Prize in 2015/16, Helen Mort said:

'When I encounter new voices so exhilarating and exact they require me to listen differently, to attend properly, it's a rare thrill. Judging the New Poets Prize yielded many such moments of surprise and delight.'

In association with Arvon. Supported by Arts Council England

Also published by smith|doorstop in the
New Poets List:

PHOEBE STUCKES, GIN & TONIC

There's a sense of confidence in these poems that won't let you rest. Each seems to tell you a secret and then make you complicit in it too. From compelling monologues to blues pieces, every poem is charged with a savage humour, building a world where 'getting dressed feels / like being stood up' and 'crying in cabs / could be glamorous / if I did it correctly.'

– Helen Mort

Gin & Tonic is about the bittersweet experience of trying to grow up fast. The poems, written whilst living alone for the first time, are about drinking and pop music, trauma and love, glitter and girls.

Phoebe Stuckes is a poet from Somerset. She has been a winner of the Foyle Young Poets award four times and is a Barbican Young Poet. She has performed at the Southbank Centre, Wenlock Poetry Festival and the Poetry Cafe, and was the Ledbury Festival young poet in residence in 2015. Her poetry has been published in *The Missing Slate*, *Rising*, *The Morning Star* and *Ambit* among others.

Gin & Tonic is published by smith|doorstop. Order it now from the shop at http://www.poetrybusiness.co.uk

THEOPHILUS KWEK, THE FIRST FIVE STORMS

The First Five Storms' has remarkable range and imaginative depth, from Fibonacci to Loch na Fuaiche, from the small detail of 'thawed streams like cracks in the bone' to a panorama of the whole 'lifting land'. These are poems that excavate, honour and renew.

– Helen Mort

Theophilus Kwek is 22 and studying for a MSc in Refugee and Forced Migration Studies in Oxford. He has published three collections of poetry, most recently Giving Ground (2016). He won the Martin Starkie Prize in 2014, the Jane Martin Prize in 2015, and the New Poets' Prize in 2016, and was recently placed Second in the Stephen Spender Prize for Poetry in Translation, 2016. Having served as President of the Oxford University Poetry Society, he is the Co-Founder of The Kindling and a Co-Editor of Oxford Poetry. Having recently arrived in a country best-known for its weather, he charts the storms of history, language, place, and tradition in *The First Five Storms*.

The First Five Storms is published by smith|doorstop
Order it now from the shop at http://www.poetrybusiness.co.uk

IMOGEN CASSELS, THE FIRE MANIFESTO

The Fire Manifesto is full of praise-poems, poems that celebrate the detail of 'the moon reflecting on the sea', the ritual of making bread, the 'scalloped edge' of land. But the praising is never naïve – many of these poems have a haunted, haunting quality too. Knowing and sorrowful, the writing is subtle, always attentive to the music of names.

– Helen Mort

Imogen Cassels is from Sheffield, and is in her second year studying English at Cambridge. In 2015 she was selected as a Young Poet on the Underground. Her poetry is published or forthcoming in *Blackbox Manifold*, *Waymaking*, *Ambit*, *The Interpreter's House*, and *Antiphon*.

Imogen Cassels' pamphlet is forthcoming from smith|doorstop. Keep a look out for it at http://www.poetrybusiness.co.uk